Countering Violent Extremism in Indonesia

Using an Online Panel Survey to Assess a Social Media Counter-Messaging Campaign

ELIZABETH BODINE-BARON, JAMES V. MARRONE,
TODD C. HELMUS, DANIELLE SCHLANG

RAND NATIONAL SECURITY RESEARCH DIVISION

For more information on this publication, visit www.rand.org/t/RRA233-1

Library of Congress Cataloging-in-Publication Data is available for this publication.
ISBN: 978-1-9774-0569-2

Published by the RAND Corporation, Santa Monica, Calif.
© Copyright 2020 RAND Corporation
RAND® is a registered trademark.

Preface

This report presents the results of an evaluation designed to assess the effects of countering violent extremism (CVE)–themed social media content used in a campaign to promote tolerance, freedom of speech, and rejection of violence in Indonesia. RAND Corporation researchers studied the effects of the campaign by recruiting a sample of Indonesian youth through Facebook and randomly assigning them to a treatment condition that exposed participants to CVE social media content or to a control condition. This report details the research design and findings and offers recommendations for improving such evaluations in the future.

In accordance with the appropriate statutes and regulations regarding human subject protection, the researchers used human-subject protection protocols for this report and its underlying research. The views represented in this report do not represent the official policy or position of the Department of State or the U.S. government.

This research was sponsored by the Global Engagement Center at the U.S. Department of State and conducted within the International Security and Defense Policy Center of the RAND National Security Research Division (NSRD), which operates the National Defense Research Institute (NDRI), a federally funded research and development center sponsored by the Office of the Secretary of Defense, the Joint Staff, the Unified Combatant Commands, the Navy, the Marine Corps, the defense agencies, and the defense intelligence enterprise.

For more information on the RAND International Security and Defense Policy Center, see www.rand.org/nsrd/isdp or contact the director (contact information is provided on the webpage).

Contents

Figures

Tables

Summary

In this report, RAND Corporation researchers provide an assessment of the effects of an online countering violent extremism (CVE) messaging campaign in Indonesia circulated on social media by a nonprofit peace-promoting organization. The campaign's goals were to increase young people's support for diverse, inclusive communities and freedom of speech and to decrease support for the use of violence in addressing grievances. The campaign content consisted of videos and images branded by two different hashtags.

Using a randomized controlled design, we recruited more than 900 Indonesian youth via Facebook and randomly assigned them to systematically observe CVE-themed content or control content each week over the course of two months. Surveys were conducted via an online portal.

The results indicate that audiences recognized and liked the CVE-themed content at levels comparable with control social media posts derived from popular Indonesian advertisement and public service announcement campaigns. Results were mixed in terms of how well audiences understood the intent of the two different CVE hashtag campaigns.

Results showed positive treatment effects at the end of the survey period regarding attitudes toward promoting inclusivity online, although the effect was the result of an unusual and sudden drop in attitudes of the participants in the control group. In addition, the effect is no longer significant in analyses controlling for baseline differences. There also were strong, significant negative treatment effects regarding respondents' attitudes toward living in separated communities.

A secondary analysis compared respondents who lived in Java, the region previously exposed to the live social media campaign, with respondents living outside Java. Results showed that the treatment effects were stronger for respondents outside Java. In this subsample, the campaign showed a significant positive treatment effect regarding views on the justification of violence and a negative treatment effect regarding attitudes toward judging others.

We conclude that the campaign was partially successful in appealing to the intended audience, communicating its messages, and having positive effects on certain attitudes. However, the negative treatment effects are evidence of possible boomerang effects, which have been found in other messaging campaigns.

We identify several lessons for future campaigns and impact evaluations. Formative research could pretest for possible boomerang effects to improve the likelihood of a positive effect on the target audience. Future impact evaluations could utilize alternative study designs to mimic more realistic exposure to campaign content. Overall, social media still offers a promising platform for CVE messaging, particularly when targeted at young people, who use social media as an important source of news and information.

Acknowledgments

We are grateful to numerous individuals and entities that supported the conduct of this research. Within the RAND Corporation, Natasha Lander and Ashley Rhoades helped with study logistics. RAND's Survey Research Group provided technical expertise for implementing the survey. Tom Conners of the University of Maryland provided extremely valuable translation skills and advice, including consultations on the survey, feedback on tech camps, and monitoring of the survey contact email. The staff at Search for Common Ground, especially Gracia Respati, were critical partners throughout the course of this research, assisting with development of survey questions and hosting RAND staff during Indonesia-based events. Other staff worked closely with RAND, including Merry Rismayani, Bahrul Wijaksana, and Moudy Sarman. Christine Hortinela at engageSPARK patiently assisted with payment of our survey respondents. We are also grateful to Timothy Andrews and Jill Moss at the Global Engagement Center for trusting RAND with this work. Finally, we would like to thank Andrew Shaver of the University of California, Merced and Erika Bloom of the RAND Corporation for helpful and insightful comments that improved the quality of this report. Any errors in this report are the sole responsibility of the authors.

Abbreviations

ANCOVA	analysis of covariance
CVE	countering violent extremism
GEC	U.S. Department of State Global Engagement Center
IFLS	Indonesia Family Life Survey
M&E	monitoring and evaluation
NSRD	National Security Research Division
PSA	public service announcement
SFCG	Search for Common Ground

CHAPTER ONE

Introduction

Violent extremism continues to threaten peace and stability in Indonesia. In 2002, the international community was awakened to this threat by the attacks against a tourist area in Bali; the attacks were committed by al Qaeda affiliate Jemaah Islamiyah.[1] The Islamic State has recently taken center stage in Indonesia, luring more than 500 Indonesians to Syria and Iraq (Barrett, 2017) and, with affiliate Jamaah Ansharut Daulah, conducting a spate of attacks in Indonesia. These incidents include a 2017 attack in East Jakarta that killed three and a 2018 attack that killed 12 (Hutton, 2017; Beech and Suhartono, 2018). There are concerns that the Islamic State will seek to increase operations in Southeast Asia to compensate for losses in the Middle East (Abuza and Clarke, 2019). Consequently, it is critical to develop strategies and efforts to reduce the lure of extremism in Indonesia.

One such strategy involves communication campaigns that promote countering violent extremism (CVE). The U.S. government, the international community, and private foundations rely on communication campaigns for their CVE efforts. For example, the U.S. Department of State previously funded the Viral Peace program, which trained civil society groups to share CVE content on social media (Ackerman, 2012). The Department of State also started what is now a Facebook-funded program called Peer to Peer, which is focused on university

---

[1] Violent extremism in Indonesia long preceded the Bali attacks. Jemaah Islamiyah killed 31 in a series of attacks in 2000. The violent extremist group Komando Jihad operated during the 1970s, and the extremist movement known as Darul Islam fought to establish an Islamist state in Indonesia during the 1940s and 1950s.

students (EdVenture Partners, undated). The U.S. Agency for International Development supports the Voices for Peace program, which seeks to amplify moderate voices of peace and tolerance in such nations as Burkina Faso, Chad, and Niger (U.S. Agency for International Development, 2018). The Gen Next Foundation helped develop and fund implementation of the Redirect Method, which uses Google's AdWord technology to serve CVE content to users who search for violent jihadist and far-right content in the United States (Helmus and Klein, 2018).

Despite the widespread use of such campaigns, research assessing the effects of CVE communication campaigns is still in its early phases (Beaghley et al., 2017). Such assessments are key to monitoring and evaluation (M&E) efforts, which help improve communications campaigns and ensure that resources go to campaigns that work.

Several studies have examined the effect of CVE radio programming in Africa (Paluck and Green, 2009; Bilali and Vollhardt, 2013; Bilali and Vollhardt, 2015); RAND researchers recently conducted a randomized controlled trial to assess the effect of a CVE-themed radio program in northern Nigeria (Marrone et al., 2020). These studies generally conclude that such programs are able to change attitudes and behaviors regarding CVE-related topics. For example, the radio program led to significant long-term improvements in attitudes about the importance of being a role model to youth (Marrone et al., 2020).

The research base is more limited for online CVE campaigns. In a review of recently published research on online CVE campaigns, Helmus and Klein (2018) found that this research rarely focused on the effects of CVE programming. Most often, M&E resources are used to assess the formative aspects of a campaign (materials under development and their relationship with the target audience) or on the campaign process (audience reach and engagement, such as likes, shares, and comments). Although these components of M&E are important, they do not gauge the effect on audience attitudes or behavior.[2] Helmus

---

[2]   As an exception to this rule, audience comments are sometimes analyzed to infer that the attitudes of some message recipients were directly affected by exposure to the campaign (Silverman et al., 2016). For an in-depth discussion on the merits of such an evaluation approach, see Helmus and Klein (2018).

and Klein concluded that "little is known" about the actual effect of online CVE campaigns on audiences' knowledge, attitudes, or behavior.

The purpose of this study was to address this critical gap in knowledge. Specifically, we sought to assess whether an online CVE campaign led to significant improvements in the attitudes of audience members. This study is part of a broader RAND portfolio of research called the RAND Countering Violent Extremism Impact Evaluation. The CVE campaign that we focus on in this report was launched in Indonesia in fall 2019. It was designed and implemented by Search for Common Ground (SFCG), a nonprofit organization that seeks to use "innovative tools to end violent conflict around the world" (SFCG, undated). Both our assessment and the SFCG campaign design and implementation were funded by the Global Engagement Center (GEC) at the U.S. Department of State.

SFCG sought to amplify the opinions of the *silent majority* through this particular online campaign. In this case, the silent majority is made up of young people who do not support intolerance and bigotry but who also might not speak out against it. SFCG chose to conduct a social media campaign partly because of the widespread usage of social media in Indonesia. More than 50 percent of Indonesians have Facebook accounts (Statcounter, undated), presenting a unique opportunity to reach audiences—particularly younger ones. There is also support for the idea that a silent majority exists. In 2013, a Pew survey found that 92 percent of the Indonesian population believed that suicide attacks were rarely or never justified (Pew Research Center, 2013). More recently, the Indonesia Survey Institute released a poll in which 82 percent of the Indonesian population were increasingly concerned about terrorism as a result of the recent rise in terror attacks; most favored more stringent antiterrorism laws. In addition, 53 percent reported that civil society organizations and institutions had not done enough to raise awareness ("Indonesians More Worried About Terrorism, Support Stronger Measures: Survey," 2018).

The campaign's goals included increased support for ethnically and religiously diverse communities, increased support for freedom of speech and religion, and decreased support for the use of violence as a solution to problems. SFCG worked with a market research firm to design content for Facebook, Instagram, Twitter, and YouTube using two different hashtags developed specifically for the campaign: *#AkuTemanmu* ("I am your friend") and *#CapekGakSih* ("Aren't you tired?").

To design an assessment of SFCG's social media content, we drew from the conclusions of Helmus and Klein (2018) to leverage promising approaches for assessing online CVE campaigns (see also Lim et al., 2016). Two broad options exist for assessing the effect of online campaigns. First, researchers can use what is referred to as an *open* design. Open designs assess live social media campaigns, frequently using pre- and postcampaign surveys to assess changes in audience knowledge, attitudes, and behavior. One benefit of open campaigns is that they draw on the rich trove of data and analytics provided by the social media platforms. This data includes audience impressions, reach, and engagement (likes, shares, and comments). However, exposure to social media content is highly self-selective (users are not passively exposed to material; they choose which content to consume). In addition, the rapid flow of social media information across browser screens can reduce the accuracy of exposure recall (Andersen, de Vreese, and Albæk, 2016; Niederdeppe, 2016; Niederdeppe, 2014; de Vreese and Neijens, 2016), making it difficult to identify the exposed audience based on survey responses.

The alternative is a *closed* design, in which researchers recruit participants especially for the study and formally expose them to the social media content, conducting follow-on surveys or other tests to assess whether exposure to the social media content produced the intended effect. A benefit of closed designs is that they can be conducted as randomized controlled trials, allowing for comparisons between a treatment group exposed to the content and a control group exposed to other content. A key limitation of closed designs is their lack of ecological validity—participants do not necessarily consume the content in the same way that they would do so while scrolling through their usual social media feeds.

We used a closed design, recruiting 1,570 participants from Indonesia via a series of Facebook advertisements. We randomly assigned participants either to a treatment group that viewed SFCG's CVE content or to a control group that viewed non-CVE placebo content. The placebo content consisted of advertisements from Indonesian entertainment media and retail companies, as well as public service announcement (PSA) campaigns. The closed design provided an evaluation of effects that complemented the formative research and process evaluation conducted by SFCG before and during the campaign itself (Maverick, 2018).

Both treatment and control group respondents viewed content on a weekly basis for two months. Four surveys measured participants' attitudes and behaviors related to SFCG's campaign goals and to some of the placebo PSA campaigns; these were conducted at enrollment, midway through the exposure period, and twice after the conclusion of the exposure period. In addition, during each week of the exposure period, the survey measured the familiarity and likeability of both treatment and placebo content. Participants were paid in mobile phone credit for each week of the survey that they completed.

Because SFCG's campaign began circulating organically on social media six months before our research started, participants in both the treatment and control group could have been exposed to the campaign content outside of the formal survey setting. However, any treatment effects in the study would be caused by exposure *beyond* what participants experienced in the course of their typical social media usage. This is a randomized encouragement design, which has been used in other settings to study radio and television programs while the programs are still on the air (Bjorvatn et al., 2015; Berg and Zia, 2017).

In our research, there are two sources of difference in exposure between the control and treatment groups. First, the panel survey amplifies the exposure of treatment group participants relative to control group participants. In addition to repeated, regular exposure on a weekly basis, respondents are asked if they can recall seeing SFCG's content on their social media feeds and about the message of each advertisement. These questions promote a higher degree of engagement than might be expected from normal social media use. Second, SFCG's campaign was circulated in Java, but survey respondents were drawn from both Java and 16 additional provinces in Indonesia. Respondents from outside Java would only see the content based on social network connections, likes, and shares, and would be expected to have a lower baseline exposure rate than respondents from Java. The analysis leverages both sources of variation in exposure.

This report contributes to the evidence base for optimal campaign design in a country where social media is an increasingly important medium for disseminating extremist beliefs (Institute for Policy Analysis of Conflict, 2015; Fealy, 2016). Given the rising popularity of social media in Indonesia, this is not surprising. In 2018, an estimated 133 million Indonesians (about 50 percent of the total population) had internet access, and 98 percent of Indonesians with internet access used social media (We Are Social, 2018). Accordingly, social media has also become an important medium for counter-narrative messaging (Silverman et al., 2016; Lee, 2019). The Indonesian government and other groups have used online campaigns as part of a broader portfolio of deradicalization and counterviolence initiatives (Qatar International Academy for Security Studies, 2013), and studies of online countermessaging's effectiveness have yielded an increasingly sophisticated understanding of how and by whom such content should be designed to maximize reach and generate sustained engagement (Helmus, York, and Chalk, 2013; Lim, 2013; Tuck and Silverman, 2016).

About This Report

The remainder of this report details our assessment methodology, findings, limitations, and recommendations. In Chapter Two, we describe the methodology, including survey design and implementation, empirical measurement strategy, and comparison to prior research. In Chapter Three, we describe the sample demographic characteristics, measures of campaign reach and resonance, and treatment effects. Finally, in Chapter Four, we highlight key takeaways, including limitations of the study, lessons learned from the research, ways to improve the social media campaign design, and recommendations for future impact evaluations. The appendixes provide information on unnormalized outcomes and robustness.

CHAPTER TWO

Methodology

SFCG Social Media Campaign and Placebo Content

SFCG worked with Maverick, an Indonesian market research firm, to conduct formative research on target audience characteristics and beliefs (Maverick, 2018). The target audience consisted of young Indonesians (ages 18–35) who were active on social media.[1] Maverick conducted focus groups and interviews to identify thematic storylines that resonated with the audience. The research identified a critical lack of peaceful, tolerant narratives circulating on social media, despite the fact that a silent majority of young people were critical of extremist and intolerant views.

To address the lack of peaceful alternatives to online intolerance, SFCG coordinated with Maverick to design the campaign around the general notion of "an encounter" (*sebuah perjumpaan*). Encountering people who are different from oneself can be an opportunity to expand one's worldview, but too often online encounters are divisive, rather than unifying. Accordingly, SFCG developed two different hashtags emphasizing different aspects of the "encounter" story. Content (including both images and videos) created for each hashtag was then circulated on Facebook, Instagram, Twitter, and YouTube. Maverick constructed sample content and tested it on social media

---

[1]   *Indonesian* refers to people residing full-time in Indonesia, not necessarily to native-born Indonesians. The World Bank estimates that 0.13 percent of Indonesia's population are immigrants, so it is likely that everyone exposed to SFCG's campaign and all of our study participants were native-born (World Bank, undated).

to measure the degree to which it was shared, liked, or commented upon. Maverick also identified potential campaign partners (peaceful messaging activists and organizations) who could share the content on their own social media profiles or create their own branded content using the same hashtags.

The first hashtag, *#CapekGakSih* ("Aren't You Tired?"), was meant to give voice to the possible feelings of the silent majority: Negative comments and posts on social media are exhausting and affect everyone, and Indonesians are united in seeking an end to online negativity (Maverick, 2018). Content created with this hashtag emphasized how different opinions or tastes are often pitted against each other, instead of seeking a middle ground. Some content also mentioned the ubiquity of fake news and disinformation. A second hashtag, *#TidakHarusPolarisasi* ("[Interactions] Don't Have to Be Polarizing"), was sometimes used in conjunction with *#CapekGakSih*. Figure 2.1 shows a sample of images used for this portion of the campaign.

The second hashtag, *#AkuTemanmu* ("I Am Your Friend"), was meant to provide an answer to the implicit question behind "aren't you tired?" by recasting online encounters as opportunities for personal growth and shared humanity. Content created with this hashtag

Figure 2.1
Sample Content from *#CapekGakSih* ("Aren't You Tired?")

SOURCE: Screenshots provided by SFCG.
NOTES: The English translations are as follows:
Left: "Housewives are labeled as not supporting emancipation / And working women are labeled as wanting a career rather than children."
Center: "Why does it have to be win/lose, if you can find a middle ground?"
Right: "Why is it easier to spread a hoax than to spread charity?"

emphasized that people of different ethnicities, religions, and lifestyles are all Indonesian. Videos were also created to provide personal stories that debunk stereotypes about particular groups and emphasize the importance of judging people based on more than their appearance. A second hashtag, *#BanggaJadiOrangIndonesia* ("Proud to be Indonesian"), sometimes accompanied the content. Figure 2.2 shows a sample of the images created for this portion of the campaign.

As explained further below, images and videos created by SFCG were used in conjunction with placebo content in our impact evaluation survey.[2] Depending on their treatment assignment, respondents were exposed to online content drawn from the following four different sets of material: (1) the *#AkuTemanmu* campaign; (2) the *#CapekGakSih* campaign; (3) commercial and entertainment ads from mainstream Indonesian media; and (4) Indonesian PSA campaign content unrelated to CVE topics. Each set of material contained a mixture of print images and videos.

Figure 2.2
Sample Content from #*AkuTemanmu* ("I Am Your Friend")

SOURCE: Screenshots provided by SFCG.
NOTES: The English translations are as follows:
Center: "266 million+ population / 17,508 islands / 700+ local languages / 300+ tribes / But only 1 official language. That can allow us to communicate with each other. / Same language. Indonesian. / Because we are the same. Indonesian people."
Right: "Different tastes in music, but still cool netizens."

---

[2]   As part of the campaign, social media influencers and nongovernmental organizations created their own content and circulated it on their social media channels with SFCG's hashtags. This third-party content was not included as part of our survey.

The two groups of placebo content were drawn from recent, highly rated advertising campaigns that had won Indonesian advertising awards or had been among the most-viewed online content. Advertisements included content for IKEA, an online travel website, a language-learning app, candy and snack food, cosmetics, computers, headphones, and Go-Jek (a local ride-sharing service). PSA topics included ecological awareness, safer driving, the benefits of exercise, discouraging public defecation, and raising awareness of child abuse.

Survey Development and Outcome Questions

During the formative market research phase of the campaign, we worked with SFCG to develop a logic model to identify measurable short- and long-term attitude and behavior outcomes. The exercise yielded the following three long-term goals: (1) increased support for freedom of speech; (2) increased support for diverse, inclusive communities; and (3) decreased support for the use of violence in everyday life. The short-term goal was to increase awareness of and concern about fake news.

To measure attitudes and behaviors related to these campaign goals, we developed a survey that asked about respondents' attitudes and behaviors. The survey also assessed the SFCG social media campaign's reach and resonance. Some questions came from a survey fielded during a tech camp held by SFCG prior to the impact evaluation, and others were written for this evaluation.[3] The tech camp provided an opportunity to pretest several potential questions in samples of roughly 30 people each, at locations around the island of Java. For other questions, SFCG and RAND conducted cognitive testing on the attitude and behavior questions, using a group of respondents of various ages and levels of education from rural and urban areas near Jakarta. Question formats and translations were revised based on feedback from the test-

---

[3] This tech camp was part of a series of tech camps meant to train young people to become social media influencers who could spread credible, self-created peaceful narratives. The tech camps were unrelated to the campaign studied here, but this camp provided an opportunity to pretest possible survey questions in a population similar to the target audience.

ing process. Some demographic information was gathered using questions that had already been tested and fielded in the Indonesia Family Life Survey (IFLS) (Strauss, Witoelar, and Sikoki, 2016). The IFLS also provides a population-level benchmark for sample characteristics.

Table 2.1 lists the outcome questions of interest. The three questions on reach and resonance provide evidence of how many people have both seen SFCG's campaign content *and* recall seeing it, as well as evidence of how much people like the content in comparison to placebo content, and whether the messages they take away from the content are similar to SFCG's intended messages.

The nine attitude and behavior questions are derived from SFCG's logic model. The first five questions ask about attitudes related to inclusivity and freedom of speech, based on Likert-scale elicitations of agreement or disagreement with a statement. Question 6 asks about how the respondent resolves disagreements, in person or online. The next two questions ask about social-media related behaviors and opinions: Question 7 asks whether a trusted source is more or less important than other considerations when sharing content, and question 8 asks whether fake news is more or less important than other topics, all of which are drawn from the placebo PSA campaigns. Question 9 asks about the use of violence and the degree to which it is justified in various situations.

For the analyses below, responses to questions 7 and 8 were reformatted into binary variables based on the distribution of answers at baseline. For question 7, the binary variable indicates that the factor is "very" or "somewhat" important. For question 8, the binary variable indicates that the respondent felt the topic was "very" important to them.

The questions are formatted in a direct way, which could raise concerns about the accuracy of responses—particularly for sensitive topics, such as the justification of violence. The format was dictated primarily by the results of cognitive testing. We tested other formats, including list experiments and endorsement experiments, that are well-suited to eliciting honest answers about sensitive topics (for examples of their effectiveness, see Blair, Imai, and Lyall, 2014). The wording and instructions for these questions, however, presented some confusion. In the context of a remote survey without human guidance, we

Table 2.1
Outcome Questions Asked in Each Follow-Up Survey

Question Category and Number	Label	Question Text [Answer format]
Campaign reach and resonance		
1	Reach	Have you seen this ad/video before? [Yes or no]
2	Resonance	How much did you like this ad/video? [Scale of 1 ("I disliked it very much") through 7 ("I liked it very much")]
3	Message	What do you think is the message of this ad/video? [Free response]
Attitudes and behaviors		
1	Judging by appearance	"People's appearances are usually an effective way to judge whether I want to get to know them."[a]
2	Separate communities	"It is best if people of different religions and ethnicities live in separate communities."[a]
3	Interacting with others	"I enjoy having conversations with people whose ideas and values are different from my own."[a]
4	Promoting inclusion	"I actively try to promote inclusivity in my daily life on social media."[a]
5	Freedom of speech	"It is important to protect freedom of speech for all individuals, even if I disagree with them."[a]
6	Response to dispute	Considering the list below, which of these options would you consider using if you had a dispute with somebody? [Check all that apply.] • remaining silent/doing nothing • talking to that person politely • responding to that person with an insult • airing my feelings on social media • responding with violence

Table 2.1—Continued

Question Category and Number	Label	Question Text [Answer format]
7	Reasons for posting	When you decide to post or share something on social media, are each of the following options very important, somewhat important, or not at all important?[b] • The content should receive a lot of "likes" from my friends. • The content should be funny or interesting. • The content should come from a source I trust. • The content should be created by me, not reposted from somebody else. • The content should contain a photo or video, not just words.
8	Comparing PSAs	For each of the following, tell us whether it is very important to you, somewhat important, or not at all important.[b] • caring for the environment • being a safe driver • caring for elderly people in my community • keeping my community clean from litter and trash • stopping the spread of fake news on social media
9	Justification of violence	For each of the following, do you think using violence would be justified? [Scale of 1 ("always") to 5 ("never")] • when my family or I am insulted • when my belief or religion is insulted • when my ethnicity is insulted • when my ideology or political opinion is insulted • when my job or livelihood is threatened • when my life or my family's life is threatened

[a] Respondent chose an option from a five-point Likert scale (1 = "strongly disagree," 2 = "somewhat disagree," 3 = "neither agree nor disagree," 4 = "somewhat agree," 5 = "strongly agree").

[b] Respondents chose an option from a three-point Likert scale for each category (1 = "very important," 2 = "somewhat important," or 3 = "not important").

felt that using these questions might introduce inaccuracy because of misunderstandings of the questions.

Direct questions have been shown to yield inaccurate answers because of social desirability bias (Rosenfeld, Imai, and Shapiro, 2015). We believe the risks are minimized by three aspects of the survey design. First, the survey was self-administered, which has generally been shown to reduce social desirability bias compared with interviewer-administered surveys (Tourangeau, Rips, and Rasinski, 2000). Second, nonresponse rates were very low. Of those who took the survey each week, less than 1 percent skipped any given question, suggesting that respondents did not find questions particularly intrusive. Still, respondents may have felt compelled to provide answers in agreement with campaign goals if they did not trust the anonymity of the survey. Finally, given the experimental design, social desirability bias is only a problem insofar as the treatment group and control group have different tendencies to misreport their true opinions. If, after seeing SFCG's content, the treatment group felt more pressure to agree with the message of the campaign, this would exaggerate the estimated treatment effect. But our estimated effects are almost all negative, with few exceptions, suggesting that another mechanism explains the results.

Study Design and Participant Recruitment

Figure 2.3 illustrates the study design. There were four stages: recruitment, baseline survey, randomized exposure, and follow-up.

Study participants were recruited using targeted Facebook ads. These ads were in Indonesian (Bahasa) and were targeted to Facebook users from ages 18 to 35 in 22 provinces. The ads offered a chance to earn mobile phone credit by sharing opinions regarding media campaigns. Fifty-eight Facebook users who saw the ads shared the ad with their own Facebook network, which further expanded the reach of the ad content. By the end of the recruitment phase, the Facebook ads had reached 762,624 unique profiles and generated 6,968 clicks.

Clicking on the Facebook ad took users to RAND's baseline survey, hosted on a separate site. This survey first screened for study

Figure 2.3
Survey Evaluation Design

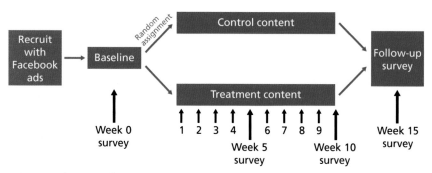

NOTE: Weeks 1–4 and 6–9 participants viewed and rated treatment or control social media content.

eligibility by asking for the participant's age and province of residence, screening out people who were under 18 or over 35, as well as people who did not live in the Indonesian provinces selected for inclusion in the study. Eligible participants were taken to a screen providing the consent form. Consent was provided digitally, and those who consented immediately took the baseline survey. The consent form indicated that participants would be asked to review marketing and social media content, and that the content they looked at would be determined randomly. They were not informed of the differences between control and treatment groups and did not know that the true purpose of the study was to evaluate SFCG's campaign.

Immediately after consenting to the study, participants completed the baseline survey. This asked about demographic information, internet and social media use, specific social media experiences, and the attitude and behavior questions listed in Table 2.1. It also collected the participant's email address and phone number for use in administering the subsequent surveys and distributing the incentive payments.

Sample size was primarily determined by budget: as large a sample as possible was desirable. Lacking any evidence for attrition in an online survey with this particular population, we opted to pay slightly larger incentives to mitigate attrition, at the expense of a slightly smaller sample. A power analysis assuming 5 percent probability of type I error and 20 percent probability of type II error (i.e., 80 percent power) showed that the minimum detectable effect size for a sample of 1,200 would be 0.14, which would be considered a small effect by one rule of thumb often used in analyses of public health messaging campaigns (Cohen, 1988).

A total of 1,929 baseline surveys were completed during the enrollment period. The baseline survey responses were then reviewed, and cases with duplicate, missing, or invalid phone numbers and/or email addresses were removed. The remaining 1,570 sample members were included in the final sample. After collecting baseline data, respondents were randomly assigned to either the treatment or control groups (based on gender and province) before taking the first follow-up survey.

After the baseline survey was completed, all subsequent survey invitations were sent by email to the address provided by the sample member; each email included an individualized link to the week's survey, with an embedded PIN to allow researchers to link each response to the specific sample member. The surveys were administered each week for ten weeks after the baseline, with a final survey administered 15 weeks after baseline. Each survey was launched on a Thursday (with the exception of holiday weeks) and closed one week later. In weeks 1–4 and 6–9, participants viewed ad images and videos and answered questions about reach and resonance. They answered questions about attitudes and behaviors in weeks 5, 10, and 15.

When participants clicked on each week's survey link, they were taken back to the survey interface. In weeks 5, 10, and 15, each question was shown on a separate screen. In weeks 1–4 and 6–9, each of the four pieces of social media content was embedded on a separate screen; participants could view images or watch videos in the survey website itself. They clicked arrows after viewing each piece of content to answer questions about it, before moving on to the next piece of content. This allowed us to verify that participants did indeed see each piece of content and to measure how long they spent on each wave of the survey.

Each sample member was sent a link to each week's survey, regardless of whether he or she had responded to the prior week's survey.

The only exceptions were 58 sample members whose email addresses were undeliverable and 142 sample members who clicked on an opt out button included in each weekly email.[4] Data quality was reviewed each week by reviewing the time it took each sample member to complete the survey and by reviewing the quality of open-ended questions. Respondents with comparatively short survey completion times were sent an email reminder of the importance of paying close attention and answering questions completely. Each week, sample members who completed that week's survey were compensated by receiving 20,000 Indonesian rupiah in mobile phone credit (approximately $1.22).

In weeks 5, 10, and 15, respondents answered the attitude and behavior questions (as shown in Table 2.1) and provided additional demographic data. The exception was question 9, which was asked at baseline and week 15 only, for reasons of survey length. The order of the attitude and behavior questions was randomized for each participant each week; for questions 6 through 9, the order of answer categories was randomized as well.

In weeks 1–4 and 6–9, respondents viewed media content according to their treatment assignment. Treatment group respondents looked at one piece of content from each of the SFCG hashtag campaigns, one mainstream entertainment or commercial media advertisement, and one PSA advertisement. Control group respondents viewed two entertainment or commercial media advertisements and two PSA advertisements. The particular choice of content from each group was randomized for each respondent, based on the set of advertisements they had not yet viewed in prior weeks. The order of advertisements was also randomized for each respondent. Each group of advertisements contained both videos and images; there were more advertisements than weeks, so no respondent saw the same content twice. Participants answered the three reach and resonance questions in Table 2.1 for each one of the four advertisements they saw.

---

[4]   Those who opted out did not receive any further links to follow-up surveys. Several people opted out each week after the baseline (the lowest number was six and the highest number was 23). Appendix B shows that our results are robust when using the sample that participated in every week.

Statistical Analysis

The sample is well-balanced at baseline, and so treatment effects are measured based on differences between the treatment and control group in each follow-up wave. The basic empirical specification is given by Equation 1, conducted for week 5, week 10, and week 15.

$$Y_i = \alpha + \beta Treatment_i + yX_i + Province_i = \epsilon_i. \qquad \text{(Eq. 1)}$$

The dummy variable indicates the individual was assigned to treatment, and the coefficient is the parameter of interest. The coefficient indicates the average difference between the treatment and control group in that week. The set of variables controls for individual characteristics for which the treatment and control groups differ on average. The fixed effect is a dummy variable capturing province-specific effects.

A secondary analysis leverages the differential rates of organic exposure to SFCG's campaign content for respondents on and outside of the island of Java. Because SFCG's campaign had been circulated online for six months before the impact evaluation began, respondents may have been exposed to the campaign content prior to enrolling in the survey. Prior exposure might attenuate treatment effects if both the treatment and control groups have been treated. However, because the campaign circulated primarily in Java, respondents from outside Java would be expected to have lower exposure prior to enrolling in this survey. Therefore, any treatment effects would presumably be stronger among the subsample of participants outside Java than the subsample in Java.

Both analyses use an ordinary least squares regression in which the outcome measure is a continuous Likert scale variable. If necessary, response scales for these outcomes were reordered so that the largest value corresponded to agreement with SFCG's campaign goals. Outcomes were then normalized relative to the control group's baseline distribution of responses, as proposed by Kling, Liebman, and Katz (2007). The regression coefficients can be interpreted in standard deviations of the control group at time zero. When the outcome is binary, the analysis uses a logit regression and reports marginal effects. Standard errors were clustered at the province/gender level, which was the level of randomization.

The primary purpose of transforming the ordinal outcomes is to provide an intuitive interpretation of treatment effects. Prior studies of media programs use this particular transformation (e.g., Banerjee et al., 2019), but alternative transformations can also offer interpretations in terms of standard deviations. For instance, Cohen's D is a normalized difference between treatment and control groups using the pooled standard deviation. It is often used in studies of public health messaging (see Clement et al., 2013, and Allara et al., 2015). A rationale for using the Kling, Liebman, and Katz (2007) approach is that it allows for measurement of differences both between groups and within groups over time. By normalizing against the control group only, rather than the pooled distribution, we can test for baseline differences between the treatment and control group as well as compare changes for each group over time; this is similar to a difference-in-difference framework. For reference, Appendix A shows the unnormalized responses to the outcome measures in each week for each subsample analyzed in the main text.

CHAPTER THREE
Findings

In this chapter, we present the study findings. The first section tabulates participant characteristics, verifying successful randomization and calculating total exposure rates over the course of the survey. The second section describes findings related to the reach and resonance of SFCG's campaign. The last section discusses the treatment effects for attitude and behavior outcomes.

Sample Demographics, Randomization, and Compliance

Of the 1,570 individuals who entered the sample frame, at least six came from each of the 22 provinces targeted for recruitment. Figure 3.1 shows the geographic distribution of participants. To maintain a balance of respondents from inside and outside Java, enrollment from the six provinces of Java was capped at about two-thirds of the target sample size, or 1,200. Ultimately, after duplicate responses were eliminated, 75 percent of the individuals in the sample were from Java.

Sample Representativeness
Of the 1,570 people who completed the baseline survey, 940 followed up by completing at least one of the next 11 surveys. This set of 940 forms the analytic sample; the 630 who never followed up are not used in the analysis below. Analysis was conducted on a week-by-week basis, for the sample that responded in each particular week ($n = 715$ to 844 for each of weeks 5, 10, 15). Appendix B provides comparative results for the sample that responded to every long survey.

Figure 3.1
Participant Location by Province

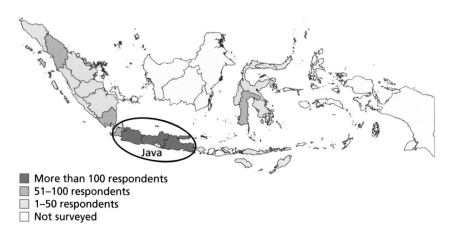

More than 100 respondents
51–100 respondents
1–50 respondents
Not surveyed

Because of the recruitment process and attrition after baseline, the analytic sample might not be representative of the population of interest (young people in Indonesia who use social media). Where possible, we compare our sample characteristics with those of the general population and to the organic audience of SFCG's campaign.

First, attrition after baseline might create selection bias. Table 3.1 highlights major differences between the baseline-only and follow-up samples. Relative to the baseline-only sample, follow-up respondents were older, more likely to live in Java, more likely to have internet at home, and used social media more heavily. (Note also that not all respondents reported having a Facebook profile, suggesting that some respondents shared the survey link privately). The follow-up sample was more likely to have accounts on the social media platforms SFCG used for the campaign; this means that the follow-up sample more closely matches the profile of the target audience but that follow-up participants might already have had heavier organic exposure to the campaign content. Apart from the question on living in separate communities, the follow-up sample had similar sentiments to the baseline-only sample on the Likert scale outcome questions of interest. There were no significant differences in any of the other outcome questions. Attrition does not affect the internal validity of the study, but it might affect external

Table 3.1
Demographic Characteristics of Follow-Up and Baseline-Only Samples

Characteristic	Baseline-Only	Follow-Up	p-Value for Difference
Female	35.8%	32.9%	0.12
Ages 18–24	60.5%	50.0%	<0.001
From Java	68.5%	80.1%	<0.001
Has internet at home	10.9%	21.5%	<0.001
Spends at least four hours per day on social media	46.3%	54.5%	<0.001
Uses Instagram	54.4%	66.5%	<0.001
Uses Facebook	90.6%	93.4%	0.02
Uses YouTube	53.1%	66.8%	<0.001
Uses Twitter	16.6%	25.9%	<0.001
Baseline outcome measures (1–5 scale)			
Judging by appearances	3.06	3.04	0.35
Separate communities	2.59	2.44	0.004
Interacting with others	1.93	1.93	0.47
Promoting inclusion	2.46	2.47	0.46
Freedom of speech	2.03	2.08	0.13

validity. Overall, Table 3.1 does suggest that our analytic sample is not representative of those who originally clicked on our recruitment ad.

To compare the analytic sample with the target population, we calculated population-level average characteristics from the IFLS for the target audience of SFCG's campaign: 18- to 35-year-olds in Java with internet access. The follow-up sample respondents from Java were more likely to be male, a student, and a high school graduate than the average 18- to 35-year-old with internet access; they were also slightly younger. They were equally likely to be Muslim and ethnically Javanese, but more likely to use Indonesian at home and less likely to use Javanese. However, in a regression on baseline responses for questions 1 through 5 in Table 2.1, none of these characteristics are significantly associated with response levels.

SFCG provided unpublished analytic data from the actual campaign to compare our survey population with actual viewers. The data comes from a small subset of the total content used for the campaign. For that content, viewership was 75 to 85 percent male and 55 to 65 percent under the age of 24. Our sample apparently had more women and older individuals than the audience of the actual campaign. Because of our recruitment strategy, we also expected our sample to have fewer individuals from Java than did SFCG's audience. However, we did not have comprehensive information on SFCG's campaign reach, including information based on geography or variation in reach over time. We therefore do not know much about the reach of the campaign before or during our survey. Our question about whether participants recognize SFCG's content is somewhat informative, but it is by no means a substitute for more comprehensive metrics from social media platforms that hosted the content. The inability to measure or control for organic exposure is a limitation that we discuss in the conclusion of this report.

Overall, the comparison to the general population and to SFCG's audience statistics indicate that our sample lies somewhere in between the two in terms of the proportion of men, the average age, and the fraction from Java. Of course, it is impossible to say how the samples differ on unobservable characteristics, including the reasons for which respondents enrolled in the first place. We discuss in the conclusion how better representativeness and lower attrition might be achieved in future studies.

Balance Check

We randomized based on gender and province, but it is important that resulting treatment and control groups be similar in terms of other observable characteristics. Table 3.2 shows the sample characteristics for the treatment and control respondents in the follow-up sample. The two groups have no statistically significant difference in characteristics or in baseline outcome measures, and the standardized differences are smaller than the threshold of 0.25 suggested by Imbens and Rubin (2015). This suggests that attrition at baseline was random with respect to treatment assignment, based on observable characteristics. The only statistically significant differences were in the responses to the outcome questions about promoting inclusivity and responding to disputes with insults. In both cases, the standardized difference is still below the 0.25 threshold.

Table 3.2 also shows that ceiling effects are not present in the ordinal outcome measures. For other outcome measures, it is possible that ceiling effects will be binding. For example, very few respondents report that they would use violence to resolve a dispute, and more than 90 percent of respondents state it is very important that they know and trust the source of any content they post on social media. Regarding the justification of violence, in most categories the average response is between five ("never") and four on a five-point scale. These outcomes at baseline mean that the magnitude of any changes in follow-up waves will be limited by the measurement scales.

Respondent Engagement and Campaign Reach and Resonance

Figure 3.2 shows the response rate for each follow-up survey wave among the 940 follow-up sample respondents. Weekly response rates were high, ranging from 70 to 90 percent, with an average around 80 percent. Participants averaged 6.45 out of eight possible weeks of content exposure (for those who did not eventually opt out, the average was 7.2 weeks).

Responses to the reach and resonance questions were grouped by advertisement category: two groups of SFCG content, entertainment or commercial media, and PSAs. Responses were aggregated over all pieces of content and all weeks. After assessing the free response answers to the question, "What is the message of this ad?," we determined that respondents who took less than two minutes to complete a survey in any given week were not sufficiently engaging with the content and were skipping through questions to get to the end. Answers from those respondents were dropped for that week and are not included in any calculations. The resulting set of data relates to 11,212 views of adver-

Table 3.2
Demographic Characteristics and Randomization Check

Characteristic	Control Mean	Treatment Mean	p-Value for Difference	Standardized Difference
Weeks of content exposure	6.5	6.4	0.29	0.036
Female	32.3%	33.5%	0.34	0.027
From Java	80.5%	79.7%	0.39	0.019
Ages 18–24	48.5%	51.5%	0.18	0.060
Speak Indonesian at home	73.9%	73.9%	0.50	<0.001
Speak Javanese at home	38.3%	40.6%	.240	0.046
Speak Sundanese at home	19.1%	21.8%	0.15	0.068
Javanese ethnicity	48.9%	52.8%	0.12	0.077
Sundanese ethnicity	21.8%	24.8%	0.14	0.070
Internet access at home	21.8%	21.2%	0.40	0.016
Internet access on phone	96.2%	95.3%	0.25	0.044
Spend at least four hours/day on social media	55.5%	53.4%	0.26	0.042
Muslim	92.8%	93.9%	0.25	0.046
Single/never married	63.7%	68.0%	0.10	0.090
Education level				
Less than high school	11.8%	10.5%	0.28	0.040
High school diploma	54.1%	55.8%	0.30	0.035
College degree	27.6%	27.1%	0.43	0.012
Less than high school, from Islamic primary school	0.7%	1.2%	0.25	0.046
Islamic high school	4.1%	3.3%	0.27	0.043
Other	0.7%	0.9%	0.37	0.024
Rural area	42.5%	42.8%	0.48	0.004
Uses Instagram	64.4%	68.6%	0.09	0.089
Uses Facebook	92.8%	94.0%	0.23	0.049

Table 3.2—Continued

Characteristic	Control Mean	Treatment Mean	p-Value for Difference	Standardized Difference
Uses YouTube	66.7%	66.9%	0.48	0.003
Uses Twitter	25.6%	26.1%	0.44	0.01
Self-rating of village safety (1–4 scale)	3.24	3.24	0.42	0.013
Student	18.3%	18.7%	0.44	0.011
Employed non-student	54.3%	50.7%	0.15	0.073
Ordinal Outcome Measures (1–5 scale)				
Judging by appearances	3.04	3.05	0.45	0.007
Separate communities	2.42	2.46	0.28	0.038
Interacting with others	1.92	1.93	0.39	0.018
Promoting inclusion	2.40	2.53	0.01	0.156
Freedom of speech	2.07	2.09	0.36	0.023
Response to disputes				
Do nothing	27.4%	21.9%	0.03	0.127
Talk	80.4%	80.6%	0.46	0.006
Insult	3.7%	6.3%	0.03	0.122
Use social media	5.4%	7.2%	0.13	0.073
Use violence	1.7%	2.1%	0.34	0.028
Reasons for Posting[a]				
Lots of "likes"	60.0%	56.0%	0.11	0.081
Funny content	84.7%	86.3%	0.25	0.045
Know the source	91.2%	91.8%	0.37	0.022
Trust the source	93.5%	94.7%	0.22	0.051
Original content	61.5%	65.1%	0.13	0.074
Contains photo/video	80.2%	79.2%	0.34	0.026

Table 3.2—Continued

Characteristic	Control Mean	Treatment Mean	p-Value for Difference	Standardized Difference
Importance of PSA Topics[b]				
Protect environment	87.1%	85.3%	0.21	0.053
Safe driving	86.0%	85.5%	0.41	0.016
Caring for elderly	77.0%	76.0%	0.36	0.023
Antilittering	85.8%	84.6%	0.31	0.033
Combating fake news	89.0%	87.2%	0.19	0.058
Justification of violence (1–5 scale)[c]				
Family/self insulted	4.11	4.07	0.28	0.037
Religion insulted	3.90	3.94	0.33	0.028
Ethnicity insulted	4.03	3.95	0.18	0.059
Politics insulted	4.22	4.15	0.17	0.062
Job threatened	4.08	4.01	0.18	0.060
Life threatened	3.48	3.41	0.25	0.045

NOTE: n = 475 (treatment) and 465 (control).

[a] Means reflect percentage of respondents who stated that the category was "somewhat important" or "very important" when posting on social media.

[b] Means reflect percentage of respondents who stated that the topic was "very important" to them.

[c] For this scale, 1 = "always justified"; 5 = "never justified".

tisements by the treatment group and 10,488 advertisements viewed by the control group.

Figure 3.3 shows the recognition rate of media content by treatment group respondents. SFCG's campaign content compares favorably with the control content, with treatment group respondents saying they recognized material in each group 36 to 39 percent of the time. The control group reported slightly higher rates of recognition for their content. In both the treatment and control groups and across all categories of content, respondents from Java reported higher rates of rec-

**Figure 3.2
Response and Compliance Rates, by Group**

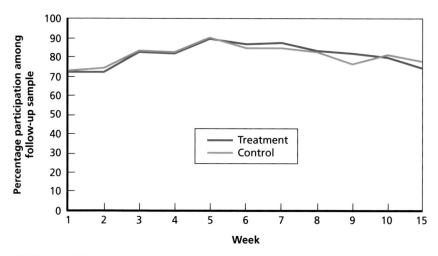

NOTE: *n* = 475 (treatment) and 465 (control).

**Figure 3.3
Recognition Rate of Media Content**

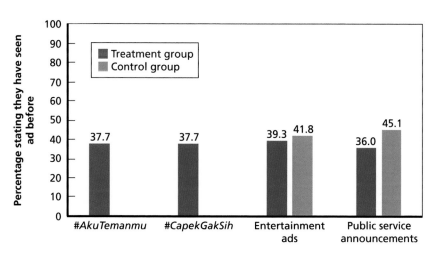

NOTE: *n* = 11,212 (treatment group) and 10,488 (control group).

ognition (by three to five percentage points), women reported lower recognition rates (by one to five percentage points), respondents who speak Indonesian at home reported higher recognition rates (by at least five percentage points), and Muslims reported higher recognition rates (by three to 10 percentage points).

For SFCG's content, respondents reported lower recognition rates for videos versus images, with a 10-percentage point gap for the *#CapekGakSih* content. The reverse was true for control content; videos had a 10- to 13-percentage point higher recognition rate than images.

Recognition of individual pieces of content varied widely. Among SFCG's content, the recognition rate varied from less than 30 percent to more than 50 percent, and it varied even more for the control content.

Figure 3.4 shows the average rating given to content from each category. The treatment group viewed SFCG's content favorably compared with the placebo content, with content created for the *#AkuTemanmu* campaign rated highest of all (and statistically significantly higher than the other groups); content for *#CapekGakSih* was rated on par with the placebo groups. Like the recognition rates, control group participants tended to rate content slightly higher than the

Figure 3.4
Average Rating of Media Content

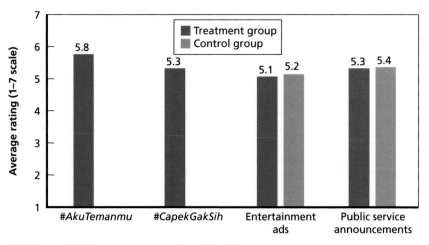

NOTE: *n* = 11,212 (treatment group) and 10,488 (control group).

treatment group (on the order of 0.1 to 0.3 points) and those who speak Indonesian at home gave significantly higher ratings. Women gave significantly higher ratings than men.

Finally, videos generally received significantly higher ratings than images, with differences in ratings of around 0.5 points. The exception was the single video for #CapekGakSih, which received a rating of 4.9 out of 7, compared with 5.4 out of 7 for the images. The video was nearly ten minutes long—much longer than other videos in the survey—and most of the respondents did not watch the entire video. The rating and viewer behavior is reflected in statistics from the actual campaign. Viewing times in the sample are on par with actual viewership times. The video was one of the most-circulated pieces of content from the campaign, with 3.8 million impression and 228,583 views. However, it also had some of the lowest numbers of shares-per-view and comments-per-view, with just 348 shares and 452 comments.

To summarize how respondents interpreted SFCG's campaign, Figure 3.5 shows word clouds for the English translations of the free-response answers to the third question about each piece of content. The word clouds suggest that respondents better grasped the message of #AkuTemanmu, using more abstract words such as "unity," "tolerance," "differences," and "diversity." The words used to describe #CapekGakSih

Figure 3.5
Word Clouds for Responses to Question: "What Is the Message of This Advertisement?" #AkuTemanmu (left) and #CapekGakSih (right)

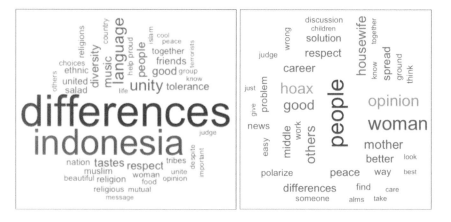

material were more concrete, reflecting the objects in the images more than the abstract message. This was particularly true of the material relating to women's roles in society, such as that on the left of Figure 2.1: "housewife," "woman," and "mother" were commonly used.

Full Sample Treatment Effects

An updated power analysis based on the actual baseline sample (and accounting for the correlation between demographic covariates and outcomes) showed that for the 940 individuals in the follow-up sample, the minimum detectable effect size was approximately 0.15, similar to the power calculated prior to recruitment.

Figure 3.6 shows the treatment effects for the five ordinal attitude and behavioral questions from Table 2.1. Results show statistically significant effects for two outcomes.

Figure 3.6
Treatment Effect for Attitude and Behavioral Questions 1–5, Full Sample

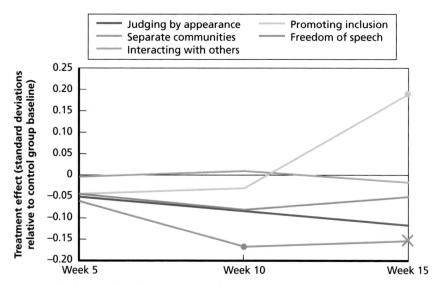

NOTES: This figure is based on RAND calculations using Equation 1 for responses to questions 1–5. Circles indicate the response was statistically significant at the 5-percent level for that week; crosses indicate significance at 10-percent level.

First, participants in the treatment group showed significant negative effects for the question on living in separate communities in weeks 10 and 15 (at the 5-percent level in week 10 and at the 10-percent level in week 15).

Second, we found a significant positive treatment effect for the question on promoting inclusion on social media. Although effects for this item were small and negative at weeks 5 and 10, the effects abruptly shifted to large and significantly positive in week 15. This effect is driven by a relatively large negative shift in the distribution of control group responses. Subsample analyses in the next subsection provide further evidence for this effect.

Figure 3.7 shows the treatment effect for the questions regarding justification of violence. This question was asked at baseline and again in week 15. A positive effect means the treatment group reported violence was relatively less justifiable, in accordance with the goals of SFCG's campaign. As a summary of responses across all categories, an aggregate index was calculated, equal to the average of the normalized z-scores of the six individual categories. The magnitudes of the effects

Figure 3.7
Treatment Effect for Question 9 (Justification of Violence), Full Sample

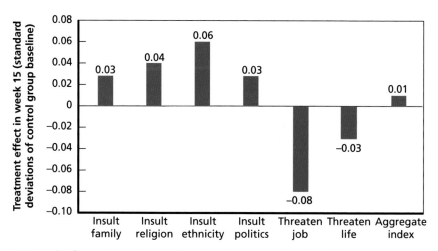

NOTES: This figure is based on RAND calculations using Equation 1 for responses to question 9 in Table 2.1. All comparisons in this table are not statistically significant.

are small, and none of the them are statistically significant. The aggregate index shows zero effect.

The treatment effects for other outcome questions show no consistent or significant pattern. Marginal effects were small, and the signs varied from week to week. Results are thus omitted from this report.

Subsample Treatment Effects

The secondary analysis compared respondents in Java separately from those outside Java. Because SFCG's campaign circulated online before the beginning of our impact evaluation, respondents might have been exposed to the campaign content prior to enrolling in the survey. Prior exposure might attenuate treatment effects if both the treatment and control groups were "treated" already. However, because the campaign circulated primarily in Java, respondents from outside Java would be expected to have lower exposure prior to enrolling in this survey. This is underscored by the recognition rates of the content; respondents outside Java reported recognition rates several percentage points lower than those in Java. Therefore, we would expect that treatment effects for the subsample of participants outside Java would be stronger than for respondents in Java.

Within each geographic subsample, ordinal questions were renormalized based on the baseline distribution of responses for the corresponding control group. Balance tests (not shown) analogous to Table 3.2 show that for each subsample there are no significant differences in average baseline responses between treatment and control groups, and the standardized differences are less than 0.25. The single exception is for the response to the question on promoting inclusion, for which the Java treatment group had significantly larger baseline responses than did the Java control group. With large differences in baseline responses, the regression Equation 1 is inappropriate; an alternative approach is necessary to control for baseline differences, such as a difference-in-difference regression or an analysis of covariance (ANCOVA) regression.

Figure 3.8 shows the treatment effects for the ordinal outcome questions among the Java response group, analogous to Figure 3.6. The dashed line provides a comparison for the question on promoting inclusion, using an ANCOVA regression that controls for respondents' opinions at baseline.[1] Within the Java response group, the question about separate communities has smaller effects that are no longer statistically significant. The question about promoting inclusion shows similar patterns, but, after controlling for baseline responses, the treatment effects are smaller and not significant.

Figure 3.9 shows the treatment effects for the same questions among the respondents from outside of Java. The sample is small and has limited statistical power though the measured effect sizes are

Figure 3.8
Treatment Effect for Attitude and Behavioral Questions 1–5, Java Subsample

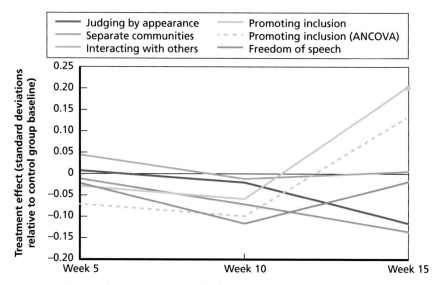

NOTES: This figure is based on RAND calculations using Equation 1 for responses to questions 1–5 from respondents in Java (*n* = 752). Circles indicate the response was statistically significant at the 5-percent level for that week.

---

[1]   The ANCOVA specification is the same as Equation 1, with the addition of the outcome measure at week 0.

Figure 3.9
Treatment Effect for Attitude and Behavioral Questions 1–5, Outside-Java Subsample

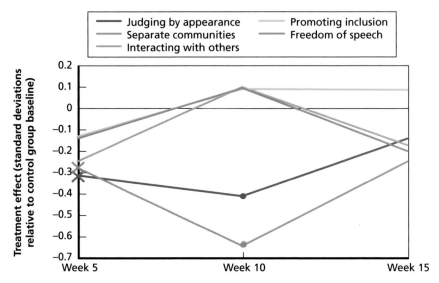

NOTES: This figure is based on RAND calculations using Equation 1 for responses to questions 1–5 from respondents outside Java (*n* = 188). Circles indicate the response was statistically significant at the 5-percent level for that week; crosses indicate significance at 10-percent level.

generally larger than for the Java-only subsample. Results show that the treatment group performed significantly worse than controls on questions on judging appearance and living in separate communities. These effects are large, around –0.3 to –0.6, and are found in weeks 5 ($p < 0.10$) and 10 ($p < 0.05$). The question on promoting inclusion shows a more moderate effect than for the Java subsample, and is not significant.

For the subsample outside Java, we did find that the treatment group reported significantly improved attitudes toward violence compared with the controls (Figure 3.10). These effects are consistently positive and moderate in size, around 0.25 to 0.35 standard deviations on the control group baseline. The aggregate effect is statistically significant at the 5-percent level, as are the individual effects for the use of violence in response to a threatened livelihood or life.

Figure 3.10
Treatment Effect for Question 9 (Justification of Violence), Outside-Java Subsample

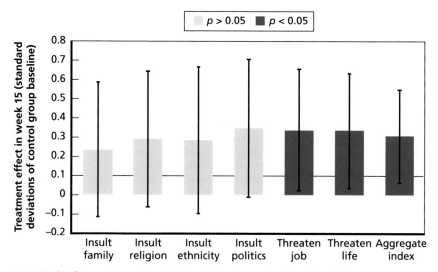

NOTES: This figure is based on RAND calculations using Equation 1 for responses to question 9 from respondents outside Java ($n = 188$). Black lines indicate 95-percent confidence intervals.

CHAPTER FOUR

Discussion and Recommendations

This report presents one of the first randomized controlled trials that assess the effects of online social media content. Several results from this study are notable.

First, more than one third of participants reported that they recognized the CVE content from both hashtags, suggesting that the live campaign reached a sizeable audience. We were not able to view the full set of campaign metrics for all of SFCG's content, so it is difficult to compare the survey findings with the live campaign's audience engagement. Future studies should couple the process evaluation data from social media platform analytics with the impact evaluation data, such as the responses to our survey.

Second, audiences reported liking the tested CVE posts at levels comparable with the mainstream advertising and PSA placebo content. This reflects well on the planning process SFCG undertook in conjunction with a market research firm and suggests that their content was effective in capturing the attention of the target audience.

Third, we documented differences in how audiences interpreted the meaning of the two hashtag campaigns. Audiences appeared to understand the meaning of the *#AkuTenmanu* campaign. Terms such as "differences," "diversity," "tolerance," and "unity" featured prominently in open-ended responses, suggesting an accurate interpretation of the campaign's intent. Audiences appeared more confused about the messages of *#CapekGakSih*. We are uncertain what effect this might have had in the treatment outcomes.

Finally, the assessment did document a significant effect between the treatment and control groups. We found a significant effect on a measure of "promoting inclusivity in daily life on social media" at week 15, five weeks after exposure to the intervention content.

It remains unclear however whether this statistically significant finding represents a positive effect of the treatment. Some indications suggest that it is not. The positive effect did not stem from any change in treatment group opinion but from a significant, abrupt drop in control group scores on this measure between weeks 10 and 15. The social media content might have helped insulate respondents in the treatment group from a change in opinion. However, the abrupt nature of the drop in control group scores weaken assertions of a positive treatment effect. The drop in scores occurred in the week of January 9 and in the week of February 9; our collaborators in Indonesia were unable to identify any geopolitical events in Indonesia that might have affected scores on this particular measure.[1] In addition, the effect is no longer statistically significant in the secondary subsample analyses after controlling for baseline differences, suggesting that it is at least partially a statistical artifact of preexisting differences in opinions between treatment and control groups.

We also found a significant and rather strong *negative* effect on feelings about living in separated (or segregated) communities and judging others' appearances. Unlike the positive effect on promoting inclusivity, these negative effects were stronger in the subsample of respondents from outside Java, who were presumably less exposed to SFCG's campaign prior to the survey.

The backfire or boomerang effect—when treatment works in the opposite direction from a campaign's goals—has been documented in health campaigns, advertising, and even entertainment programs (see Byrne and Hart, 2009, for a review). Such negative effects have also been observed in CVE campaigns. A recent RAND evaluation of a radio CVE campaign in Nigeria showed that the programming pro-

---

[1] Notably, fears of coronavirus disease 2019 do not seem a likely explanatory factor for this backlash against inclusivity because the country did not report its first case until March (Rochmyaningsih, 2020).

duced long-term positive attitudes about mentorship (Marrone et al., 2020). However, when the authors analyzed a subgroup of participants who liked and watched a significant share of the radio programs, treatment participants were less likely to report empathy for Nigeria kidnap victims, one of several key goals for the program, compared with controls. A more significant example of a boomerang effect comes from a study by Elizabeth Levy Paluck (2010). She tested the effects of a talk show in the Eastern Democratic Republic of Congo that encouraged listeners to "consider tolerant opinions and outgroup perspectives." However, she found however that the talk show led audiences to be more intolerant, less likely to aid disliked community members, and more mindful of grievances.

Byrne and Hart (2009) identify a number of explanatory theories for the boomerang effect. One theory that may apply to CVE campaigns is *reactance*. If media content attacks an audience member's strongly held belief, then that audience member might resist the message by becoming angry or feeling threatened. The message might also evoke a defensive response or argument in the mind of an audience member, and this response could reinforce and strengthen pre-existing views. However, it is unclear if reactance explains the negative outcomes in the present study. It might also be that such campaigns raise complex and uncomfortable topics with audiences, which promote cognitive attention—and, at times, rejection.

Negative outcomes do not necessarily imply that a messaging campaign was completely unsuccessful, as other components of the campaign could create positive outcomes. Policymakers must weigh such negative outcomes in the context of a program's benefits. However, in the case of this program, it appears that the negative effects might outweigh the positive effects. As noted, the negative outcomes on the "separate communities" and the "judging appearances" outcomes were rather large and occurred in a sample that might have already been exposed to the SFCG campaign. In theory, this possible previous exposure would attenuate, not strengthen, effects. The positive effects on reductions in support for violence found in the subsample were, in contrast, relatively small and occurred in a sample that had probably *not* been previously exposed to the SFCG campaign. Again, in theory, this should have strengthened results, not attenuated them. Ultimately, the mixed treatment effects documented for this campaign demand that researchers continue to investigate the effects of online CVE campaigns. It also highlights the importance of in robust pre-testing to identify such negative reactions in advance of a full messaging campaign.

Limitations and Lessons for Future CVE Assessments

Survey Accuracy

We documented some falsified survey data, including participation in the baseline survey from separate accounts that likely belonged to the same individual. Several factors increase the possibility of falsified responses: creating the sample frame through social media (not in person), conducting the study in a low-income country, and offering monetary compensation. We removed duplicate phone numbers and email addresses at baseline, but it is possible that a small number of survey participants used unique email addresses and phone numbers to complete the survey multiple times. More-robust methods of checking for duplicate sample members, such as gathering additional personally identifiable information or asking verification questions before each wave of the survey, could be used in future studies.

Some sample members may have clicked through the survey without fully reading questions or considering responses. This would result in low data quality. We tried to counteract this by checking survey response times, sending prompting emails, and reviewing open-ended responses for completeness and sense. Additional checks and enforcement mechanisms could be helpful, such as minimum times for screens showing media content and attention checks consisting of simple commands (e.g., "click the left arrow to continue," "enter the password on the last screen.")

In addition, it would be desirable to use alternative question formats, such as list experiments or randomization experiments, for sensitive topics. These might reduce any social desirability bias or outright dishonest answers. However, we believe these would be best administered by an interviewer, who could provide clear guidance on how to answer the questions.

The survey design might also generate priming effects, if participants (particularly in the treatment group) associated the social media content with each week's survey emails. Their responses to survey questions could be affected by the emotions triggered by the memory of the survey content, which would mean the measured treatment effects were influenced by the mode of delivery. One virtue of priming is that it works in favor of finding large treatment effects, similar to asking respondents to think about the message of the treatment content, which they might not do when consuming content organically. Even if priming effects are present, we found mixed evidence of the campaign's effectiveness. Alternative approaches could test for treatment effects in a more natural environment—for example, by following up using a different method and measuring outcomes using a different set of questions (for an example, see Halperin et al., 2013).

Evaluation Design

To our knowledge, this is the first randomized controlled trial of CVE social media content. Given our findings of a boomerang effect, one improvement to the survey would be to test for the potential causes of such an effect. For example, after viewing social media content, participants could be surveyed on the feelings that resulted from viewing the ad. This is one way of testing for reactance, as noted in a methodological review by Quick (2012). Such questions could provide more context for treatment effects and suggest potential mechanisms behind those effects.

The survey design also has its limitations. As noted in the introduction, we chose a closed design. It afforded the opportunity to recruit the participants that the campaign itself was targeting, it allowed random assignment of participants to treatment conditions, and it allowed control over exposure to messaging content. However, closed design has a tradeoff: The systematic exposure of content to participants does not replicate the real interaction that audiences would typically have with online content.

Another limitation—one that would not solved by an open design—is the possibility of prior or ongoing exposure to SFCG's campaign. The inferred treatment effect of the campaign is attenuated toward zero if the control group is also exposed to the campaign during the survey or if participants were already exposed and had internalized the messages of the campaign before the survey started. We did not have good data on the reach of SFCG's campaign or the probable outside exposure of our survey participants to SFCG's content.

Several alternatives exist to the current design. These alternatives would maintain the authenticity of content interaction and, in some cases, control for exposure to the campaign itself.

First, it is possible to randomly assign participants to receive content directly to their Facebook feeds. Napolitano et al. (2013), for example, tested the effect of Facebook and text messaging in delivering a weight-loss program to college students. They randomly assigned participants to a private, generically named Facebook group; a group that included a Facebook group, text messages, and personalized feedback; and a waitlist group, which served as the control. Surveys tested the effects. In applying this approach to a messaging campaign, participants would have to turn on notifications for the group so that group messages will appear in their regular Facebook feed. This approach is similar to our design in that it identifies treatment effects based on exposure above and beyond the baseline campaign.

An alternative approach would be to use Facebook advertising. Facebook permits advertisers to send posts directly to a customized audience list. Consequently, it is possible to deliver treatment and control Facebook advertisements directly to participant feeds. Pre- and postcampaign surveys could assess effect.

Second, it is possible to conduct pre- and postcampaign surveys to assess the effects of live campaigns. For example, Gough et al. (2017) tested a campaign aimed at improving attitudes and behavior toward skin cancer prevention in Northern Ireland. The campaign used promotional tweets, tweets by a cultivated group of influencers, and a Thunderclap campaign in which users allowed their social media accounts to automatically post campaign-generated messages. For the assessment, researchers used Twitter ads to recruit 337 survey participants before the campaign and 429 participants after the campaign. Analysis of survey results suggested the campaign significantly improved knowledge of skin cancer prevention and audience attitudes. A key factor in a positive treatment effect was the significant reach achieved by the campaign's robust dissemination strategy: The research team documented 417,678 tweet impressions, 11,213 engagements (message clicks, likes, comments), and 1,211 retweets. Researchers estimated that their campaign reached 23 percent of the population of Northern Ireland. This design, and the Facebook approaches mentioned earlier, avoid the possible confounding problem of prior exposure because surveys would coincide with the beginning of the campaign.

Finally, linguistic analysis of social media data might be able to detect campaign effects. William Marcellino pioneered a new approach to analysis of information operations by developing what he referred to as *resonance analysis*. Resonance analysis works by identifying the distinct language in a group's communications and quantifying the uptake of that language in the general population's social media use—whether people are talking more like the content of a tested communication campaign. Marcellino et al. (2017) tested this approach by quantifying the linguistic patterns inherent in communiques of the Islamic State. They compared the linguistic patterns of this content with a longitudinal sample of tweets from 2014 geoinferenced to Egypt. They found that over the course of 2014, an increasing number of Twitter users in upper Egypt and the Sinai (but not Cairo and Alexandria) began to adopt Islamic State linguistic patterns. Helmus et al. (2018) also used this technique to demonstrate the increasing adoption of Russian propaganda narratives in Eastern Europe.

Ultimately, numerous options exist for evaluating the effects of CVE social media content on audience knowledge, attitudes, and behavior. As governments and institutions continue to rely on social media based campaigns to disseminate CVE content, it will be critical to use a variety of rigorous evaluation techniques to establish the evidence base for what works.

Unnormalized Outcomes

Average Outcome Responses, by Week

Figures A.1 through A.6 show the average response for each outcome of interest during each week. The figures show comparisons between the three samples analyzed in this report: the full follow-up sample, the follow-up sample from Java, and the follow-up sample from outside Java. Responses are not formatted as used in the analysis, but rather are averaged in their original five-point Likert scale format, reordered when necessary so that the score of five corresponds to agreement with SFCG's thematic goals.

Figure A.1
Average Response to Question "Judging Appearances,"
by Week and Subsample

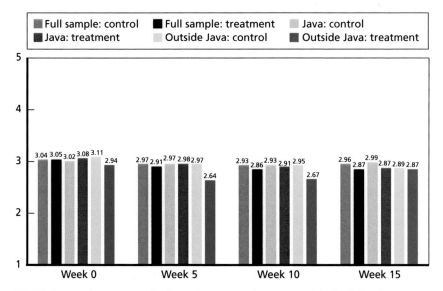

NOTES: Respondents were asked to what extent they agree with the following statement: "People's appearances are usually an effective way to judge whether I want to get to know them." 5 = "strongly disagree."

Figure A.2
Average Response to Question "Separate Communities,"
by Week and Subsample

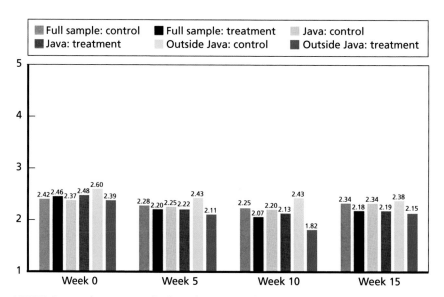

NOTES: Respondents were asked to what extent they agree with the following statement: "It is best if people of different religions and ethnicities live in separate communities." 5 = "strongly disagree."

Figure A.3
Average Response to Question "Interacting with Others," by Week and Subsample

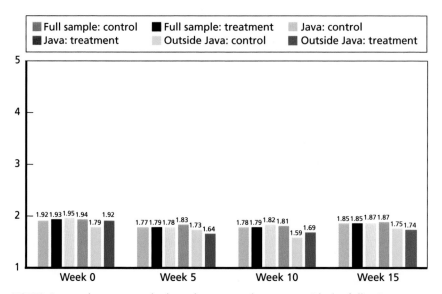

NOTES: Respondents were asked to what extent they agree with the following statement: "I enjoy having conversations with people whose ideas and values are different from my own." 5 = "strongly agree."

Figure A.4
Average Response to Question "Promoting Inclusion,"
by Week and Subsample

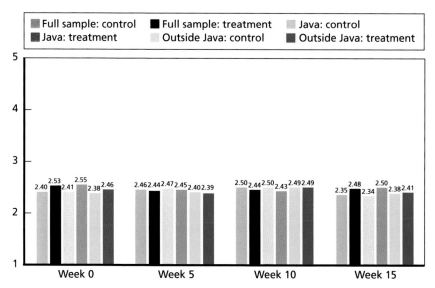

NOTES: Respondents were asked to what extent they agree with the following statement: "I actively try to promote inclusivity in my daily life on social media." 5 = "strongly agree."

Figure A.5
Average Response to "Freedom of Speech," by Week and Subsample

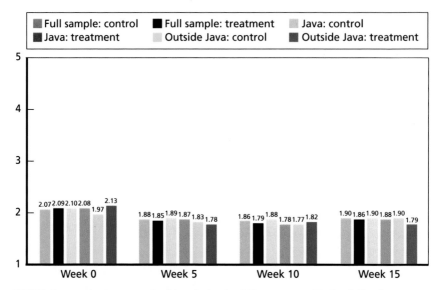

NOTES: Respondents were asked to what extent they agree with the following statement: "It is important to protect freedom of speech for all individuals, even if I disagree with them." 5 = "strongly agree."

Figure A.6
Average Response to Question: "For Each of the Following, Do You Think Using Violence Would Be Justified?," by Week and Subsample

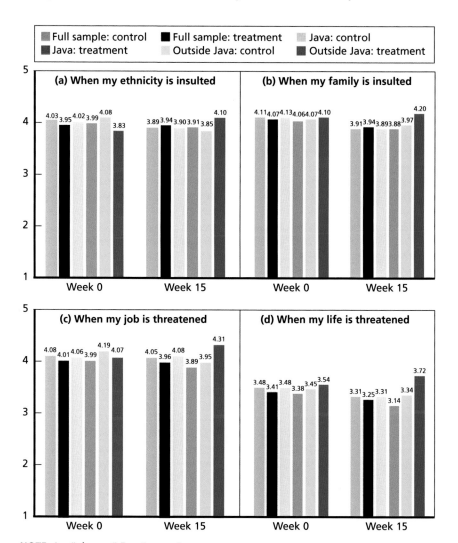

NOTE: 1 = "always." 5 = "never."

Figure A.6—Continued

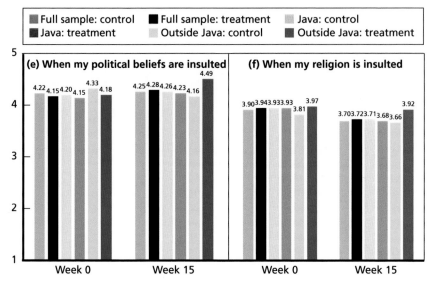

NOTE: 1 = "always." 5 = "never."

Robustness Checks

This section presents results for the sample of participants who responded to all long surveys (weeks 0, 5, 10, and 15). We call this the high-compliance sample. This sample responded to an average of 7.2 out of eight possible weeks of short surveys, so they had a high degree of exposure to the content being studied. We normalize ordinal outcomes relative to the baseline distribution of control participants in this subsample, rather than using the full sample distribution, as in the main text. For this subsample of 590 respondents, the minimum detectable effect size with 5 percent; the probability of Type I error is 0.2, slightly higher than for the full sample.

Table B.1 shows that the treatment and control group are well-balanced on observable characteristics. This means compliance was evenly balanced by observable characteristics. It also means we can use the same analytic methods as above, without controlling for baseline differences.

We then estimated treatment effects based using renormalized outcomes, in which the normalization is now relative to the baseline distribution of control participants in this subsample. Figure B.1 shows the treatment effects for the ordinal outcomes. The patterns are similar to those for the full sample (Figure 3.6). The magnitudes are slightly larger in both positive and negative directions, as would be expected if exposure to the treatment content is indeed driving the effects. Yet due to the lower power the larger effects are not statistically significant, except for the question on promoting inclusion at week 15 (as it was for

Table B.1
Demographic Characteristics and Randomization Check for High-Compliance Subsample

Characteristic	Control Mean	Treatment Mean	*p*-Value for Difference	Standardized Difference
Weeks of content exposure	7.3	7.2	0.43	0.015
Female	33.6%	33.0%	0.44	0.012
From Java	82.4%	80.9%	0.32	0.038
Ages 18–24	53.0%	61.1%	0.02	0.165
Speak Indonesian at home	85.1%	82.3%	0.18	0.076
Speak Javanese at home	46.4%	43.8%	0.26	0.052
Speak Sundanese at home	22.2%	21.5%	0.42	0.016
Javanese ethnicity	58.9%	55.2%	0.18	0.075
Sundanese ethnicity	22.5%	27.8%	0.07	0.121
Internet access at home	22.8%	26.0%	0.18	0.074
Internet access on phone	95.7%	95.5%	0.45	0.010
Spend at least four hours/day on social media	52.3%	60.1%	0.03	0.156
Muslim	94.0%	93.8%	0.44	0.012
Single/never married	64.2%	60.8%	0.19	0.072
Education level				
Less than high school	10.9%	8.3%	0.14	0.088
High school diploma	54.0%	58.0%	0.16	0.081
College degree	28.5%	29.9%	0.36	0.030
Less than high school, from Islamic primary school	1.3%	0.3%	0.10	0.107
Islamic high school	3.6%	2.4%	0.20	0.071
Other	1.3%	0.7%	0.22	0.063
Rural area	47.0%	34.7%	0.001	0.252
Uses Instagram	65.2%	72.9%	0.02	0.167

Table B.1—Continued

Characteristic	Control Mean	Treatment Mean	p-Value for Difference	Standardized Difference
Uses Facebook	94.4%	94.4%	0.49	0.003
Uses YouTube	67.5%	68.1%	0.45	0.011
Uses Twitter	25.5%	30.2%	0.10	0.105
Self-rating of village safety (1–4 scale)	3.23	3.24	0.40	0.020
Student	17.2%	14.9%	0.23	0.062
Employed nonstudent	51.3%	57.6%	0.06	0.127
Ordinal outcome measures (1–5 scale)				
Judging by appearances	3.00	3.03	0.35	0.031
Separate communities	2.36	2.35	0.46	0.007
Interacting with others	1.92	1.88	0.25	0.056
Promoting inclusion	2.41	2.54	0.02	0.163
Freedom of speech	2.07	2.07	0.48	0.004
Response to disputes				
Do nothing	26.9%	21.5%	0.06	0.126
Talk	83.4%	82.6%	0.40	0.020
Insult	3.0%	4.9%	0.12	0.096
Use social media	5.3%	7.6%	0.13	0.094
Use violence	1.7%	1.4%	0.39	0.022
Reasons for posting				
Lots of "likes"	57.6%	57.3%	0.47	0.007
Funny content	86.1%	86.5%	0.45	0.011
Know the source	91.7%	92.7%	0.33	0.037
Trust the source	94.0%	95.8%	0.16	0.082
Original content	62.9%	66.3%	0.19	0.071

Table B.1—Continued

Characteristic	Control Mean	Treatment Mean	p-Value for Difference	Standardized Difference
Contains photo/video	78.8%	80.2%	0.34	0.035
Importance of PSA topics				
Protect environment	87.7%	84.7%	0.14	0.088
Safe driving	87.7%	84.4%	0.12	0.097
Caring for elderly	78.5%	76.4%	0.27	0.050
Antilittering	87.7%	84.4%	0.12	0.097
Combating fake news	90.7%	85.4%	0.02	0.164
Justification of violence (1–5 scale)[a]				
Family/self insulted	4.09	4.06	0.39	0.023
Religion insulted	3.92	3.88	0.37	0.028
Ethnicity insulted	4.09	3.95	0.08	0.116
Politics insulted	4.19	4.17	0.43	0.014
Job threatened	4.10	4.00	0.17	0.080
Life threatened	3.48	3.45	0.41	0.018

NOTES: n = 288 (treatment) and n = 302 (control). See notes for Table 3.2 for additional details.

[a] For this scale, 1 = "always"; 5 = never.

the full sample). The question on separate communities is marginally significant at week 15.

Figure B.2 shows the treatment effects for the question about using violence. The effects are small and comparable with those for the full sample (Figure 3.7). The exception is for defending one's job, which has an effect almost double that of the full sample, although it is not significant at the 5-percent level.

**Figure B.1
Treatment Effects for Attitude and Behavioral Questions, High-Compliance
Sample**

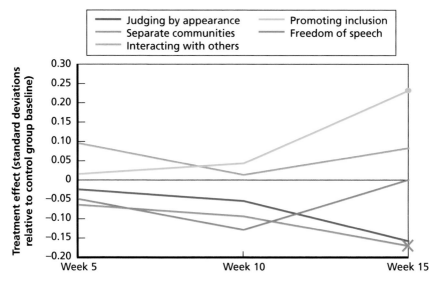

NOTES: Figure is analogous to Figure 3.6. Circles indicate the response was statistically significant at the 5-percent level for that week; crosses indicate significance at 10-percent level.

Figure B.2
Treatment Effect for Question 9 (Justification of Violence),
High-Compliance Subsample

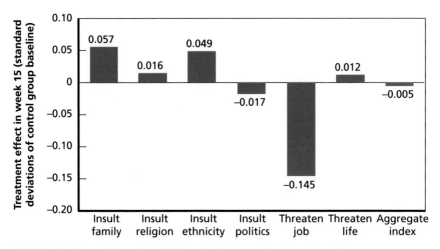

NOTES: This figure is based on RAND calculations using Equation 1 for responses to question 9 in Table 2.1. This figure is analogous to Figure 3.7. Effects are not statistically significant at the 5-percent level.

References

Abuza, Zachary, and Colin P. Clarke, "The Islamic State Meets Southeast Asia," *Foreign Affairs*, September 16, 2019. As of June 25, 2019:
https://www.foreignaffairs.com/articles/southeast-asia/2019-09-16/islamic-state-meets-southeast-asia

Ackerman, Spencer, "Newest U.S. Counterterrorism Strategy: Trolling," *Wired*, July 18, 2012. As of July 21, 2020:
https://www.wired.com/2012/07/counterterrorism-trolls

Allara, Elias, Marica Ferri, Alessandra Bo, Antonio Gasparrini, and Fabrizio Faggiano, "Are Mass-Media Campaigns Effective in Preventing Drug Use? A Cochrane Systematic Review and Meta-Analysis," *BMJ Open*, Vol. 5, No. 9, 2015.

Andersen, Kim, Claes H. de Vreese, and Eric Albæk, "Measuring Media Diet in a High-Choice Environment—Testing the List-Frequency Technique," *Communication Methods and Measures*, Vol. 10, Nos. 2–3, 2016, pp. 81–98.

Banerjee, Abhijit, Eliana La Ferrara, and Victor H. Orozco-Olvera, "The Entertaining Way to Behavioral Change: Fighting HIV with MTV," Cambridge, Mass.: National Bureau of Economic Research, 2019.

Barrett, Richard, *Beyond the Caliphate: Foreign Fighters and the Threat of Returnees*, New York: Soufan Group, 2017. As of August 10, 2020:
https://thesoufancenter.org/wp-content/uploads/2017/11/Beyond-the-Caliphate-Foreign-Fighters-and-the-Threat-of-Returnees-TSC-Report-October-2017-v3.pdf

Beaghley, Sina, Todd C. Helmus, Miriam Matthews, Rajeev Ramchand, David Stebbins, Amanda Kadlec, and Michael A. Brown, *Development and Pilot Test of the RAND Program Evaluation Toolkit for Countering Violent Extremism*, Santa Monica, Calif.: RAND Corporation, RR-1799-DHS, 2017. As of March 24, 2020:
https://www.rand.org/pubs/research_reports/RR1799.html

Beech, Hannah, and Muktita Suhartono, "At the Heart of Indonesia Terror Attacks, a Well-Liked Family," *New York Times*, May 18, 2018. As of June 25, 2020:
https://www.nytimes.com/2018/05/18/world/asia/indonesia-surabaya-terrorism-dita-oepriarto.html

Berg, Gunhild, and Bilal Zia, "Harnessing Emotional Connections to Improve Financial Decisions: Evaluating the Impact of Financial Education in Mainstream Media," *Journal of the European Economic Association*, Vol. 15, No. 5, October 2017, pp. 1025–1055.

Bilali, Rezarta, and Johanna Ray Vollhardt, "Priming Effects of a Reconciliation Radio Drama on Historical Perspective-Taking in the Aftermath of Mass Violence in Rwanda," *Journal of Experimental Social Psychology*, Vol. 49, No. 1, January 2013, pp. 144–151.

———, "Do Mass Media Interventions Effectively Promote Peace in Contexts of Ongoing Violence? Evidence from Eastern Democratic Republic of Congo," *Peace and Conflict: Journal of Peace Psychology*, Vol. 21, No. 4, November 2015, pp. 604–620.

Bjorvatn, Kjetil, Alexander W. Cappelen, Linda Helgesson Sekei, Erik Ø. Sørensen, and Bertil Tungodden, *Teaching Through Television: Experimental Evidence on Entrepreneurship Education in Tanzania*, Bergen, Norway: Norwegian School of Economics Discussion Paper, March 2015.

Blair, Graeme, Kosuke Imai, and Jason Lyall, "Comparing and Combining List and Endorsement Experiments: Evidence from Afghanistan," *American Journal of Political Science*, Vol. 58, No. 4, October 2014, pp. 1043–1063.

Byrne, Sahara, and Philip Solomon Hart, "The Boomerang Effect: A Synthesis of Findings and a Preliminary Theoretical Framework," *Annals of the International Communication Association*, Vol. 33, No. 1, 2009, pp. 3–37.

Clement, Sarah, Francesca Lassman, Elizabeth Barley, Sara Evans-Lacko, Paul Williams, Sosei Yamaguchi, Mike Slade, Nicolas Rüsch, and Graham Thornicroft, "Mass Media Interventions for Reducing Mental Health-Related Stigma," *Cochrane Database of Systematic Reviews*, Vol. 7, 2013.

Cohen, Jacob, *Statistical Power Analysis for the Behavioral Sciences*, New York: Routledge, 1988.

de Vreese, Claes H., and Peter Neijens, "Measuring Media Exposure in a Changing Communications Environment," *Communication Methods and Measures*, Vol. 10, Nos. 2–3, 2016, pp. 69–80.

EdVenture Partners, "Past Success: Peer to Peer: Facebook Global Challenge," webpage, undated. As of July 21, 2020: https://www.edventurepartners.com/peer-to-peer-facebook-global-digital-challenge

Fealy, Greg, *Indonesian and Malaysian Support for the Islamic State*, Arlington, Va.: Management Systems International, 2016.

Gough, Aisling, Ruth F. Hunter, Oluwaseun Ajao, Anna Jurek, Gary McKeown, Jun Hong, Elmear Barrett, Marbeth Ferguson, Gerry McElwee, Miriam McCarthy, and Frank Kee, "Tweet for Behavior Change: Using Social Media for the Dissemination of Public Health Messages," *JMIR Public Health and Surveillance*, Vol. 3, No. 1, 2017.

Halperin, Eran, Roni Porat, Maya Tamir, and James J. Gross, "Can Emotion Regulation Change Political Attitudes in Intractable Conflicts? From the Laboratory to the Field," *Psychological Science*, Vol. 24, No. 1, 2013, pp. 106–111.

Helmus, Todd C., Elizabeth Bodine-Baron, Andrew Radin, Madeline Magnuson, Joshua Mendelsohn, William Marcellino, Andriy Bega, and Zev Winkelman, *Russian Social Media Influence: Understanding Russian Propaganda in Eastern Europe*, Santa Monica, Calif.: RAND Corporation, RR-2237-OSD, 2018. As of April 1, 2020:
https://www.rand.org/t/RR2237.html

Helmus, Todd C., and Kurt Klein, *Assessing Outcomes of Online Campaigns Countering Violent Extremism: A Case Study of the Redirect Method*, Santa Monica, Calif.: RAND Corporation, RR-2813-GNF, 2018. As of March 23, 2020:
https://www.rand.org/t/RR2813.html

Helmus, Todd C., Erin York, and Peter Chalk, *Promoting Online Voices for Countering Violent Extremism*, Santa Monica, Calif.: RAND Corporation, RR-130-OSD, 2013. As of July 21, 2020:
https://www.rand.org/t/RR130.html

Hutton, Jeffrey, "Suicide Bombers Strike Jakarta, Killing 3 Police Officers," *New York Times*, May 25, 2017. As of June 25, 2020:
https://www.nytimes.com/2017/05/25/world/asia/indonesia-jakarta-suicide-bombings.html

Imbens, Guido W., and Donald B. Rubin, *Causal Inference for Statistics, Social, and Biomedical Sciences*, Cambridge: Cambridge University Press, 2015.

"Indonesians More Worried About Terrorism, Support Stronger Measures: Survey," *Jakarta Post*, July 31, 2018. As of June 25, 2020:
https://www.thejakartapost.com/news/2018/07/31/indonesians-more-worried-about-terrorism-support-stronger-measures-survey.html

Institute for Policy Analysis of Conflict, *Online Activism and Social Media Usage Among Indonesian Extremists*, Jakarta, October 30, 2015. As of July 21, 2020:
https://tile.loc.gov/storage-services/service/gdc/gdcovop/2017344099/2017344099.pdf

Kling, Jeffrey R., Jeffrey B. Liebman, and Lawrence F. Katz, "Experimental Analysis of Neighborhood Effects," *Econometrica*, Vol. 75, No. 1, January 2007, pp. 83–119.

Lee, Benjamin J., "Informal Countermessaging: The Potential and Perils of Informal Online Countermessaging," *Studies in Conflict and Terrorism*, Vol. 42, Nos. 1–2, 2019, pp. 161–177.

Lim, Megan S. C., Cassandra J. C. Wright, Elise R. Carrotte, and Alisa E. Pedrana, "Reach, Engagement, and Effectiveness: A Systematic Review of Evaluation Methodologies Used in Health Promotion Via Social Networking Sites," *Health Promotion Journal of Australia*, Vol. 27, No. 3, 2016, pp. 187–197.

Lim, Merlyna, "Many Clicks but Little Sticks: Social Media Activism in Indonesia," *Journal of Contemporary Asia*, Vol. 43, No. 4, 2013, pp. 636–657.

Marcellino, William M., Kim Cragin, Joshua Mendelsohn, Andrew Micahel Cady, Madeline Magnuson, and Kathleen Reedy, "Measuring the Popular Resonance of Daesh's Propaganda," *Journal of Strategic Security*, Vol. 10, No. 1, 2017, pp. 32–52.

Marrone, James V., Todd C. Helmus, Elizabeth Bodine-Baron, and Christopher Santucci, *Countering Violent Extremism in Nigeria: Using a Text-Message Survey to Assess Radio Programs*, Santa Monica, Calif.: RAND Corporation, RR-4257-DOS, 2020. As of March 23, 2020:
https://www.rand.org/t/RR4257.html

Maverick, *Search for Common Ground Peaceful Narrative Campaign*, Jakarta, unpublished research, 2018.

Napolitano, Melissa A., Sharon Hayes, Gary G. Bennett, Allison K. Ives and Gary D. Foster, "Using Facebook and Text Messaging to Deliver a Weight Loss Program to College Students," *Obesity*, Vol. 21, No. 1, 2013, pp. 25–31.

Niederdeppe, Jeff, "Conceptual, Empirical, and Practical Issues in Developing Valid Measures of Public Communication Campaign Exposure," *Communication Methods and Measures*, Vol. 8, No. 2, 2014, pp. 138–161.

———, "Meeting the Challenge of Measuring Communication Exposure in the Digital Age," *Communication Methods and Measures*, Vol. 10, Nos. 2–3, 2016, pp. 170–172.

Paluck, Elizabeth Levy, "Is It Better Not to Talk? Group Polarization, Extended Contact, and Perspective Taking in Eastern Democratic Republic of Congo," *Personality and Social Psychology Bulletin*, Vol. 36, No. 9, 2010, pp. 1170–1185.

Paluck, Elizabeth Levy, and Donald P. Green, "Deference, Dissent, and Dispute Resolution: An Experimental Intervention Using Mass Media to Change Norms and Behavior in Rwanda," *American Political Science Review*, Vol. 103, No. 4, November 2009, pp. 622–644.

Pew Research Center, "The World's Muslims: Religion, Politics, and Society," webpage, April 30, 2013. As of June 25, 2020:
https://www.pewforum.org/2013/04/30/the-worlds-muslims-religion-politics-society-overview

Qatar International Academy for Security Studies, *Countering Violent Extremism: The Counter-Narrative Study*, Doha, 2013. As of July 21, 2020:
https://qiass.org/wp-content/uploads/2016/05/CVE-Counter-Narrative-Study.pdf

Quick, Brian L., "What Is the Best Measure of Psychological Reactance? An Empirical Test of Two Measures," *Health Communication*, Vol. 27, No. 1, 2012, pp. 1–9.

Rochmyaningsih, Dyna, "Indonesia Finally Reports Two Coronavirus Cases. Scientists Worry It Has Many More," *Science*, March 3, 2020. As of August 10, 2020:
https://www.sciencemag.org/news/2020/03/
indonesia-finally-reports-two-coronavirus-cases-scientists-worry-it-has-many-more

Rosenfeld, Bryn, Kosuke Imai, and Jacob N. Shapiro, "An Empirical Validation Study of Popular Survey Methodologies for Sensitive Questions," *American Journal of Political Science*, Vol. 60, No. 3, 2015, pp. 783–802.

Search for Common Ground, "About Us," webpage, undated. As of July 21, 2020:
https://www.sfcg.org/about-us/

Silverman, Tanya, Christopher J. Stewart, Zahed Amanullah, and Jonathan Birdwell, *The Impact of Counter-Narratives: Insights from a Year-Long Cross-Platform Pilot Study of Counter-Narrative Curation, Targeting, Evaluation and Impact*, London: Institute for Strategic Dialogue, 2016.

Statcounter, "Social Media Stats in Indonesia," webpage, undated. As of June 25, 2020:
https://gs.statcounter.com/social-media-stats/all/indonesia

Strauss, John, Firman Witoelar, and Bondan Sikoki, *The Fifth Wave of the Indonesia Family Life Survey: Overview and Field Report*, Vol. 1, Santa Monica, Calif.: RAND Corporation, WR-1143/1-NIA/NICHD, 2016. As of July 21, 2020:
https://www.rand.org/pubs/working_papers/WR1143z1.html

Tourangeau, Roger, Lance J. Rips, and Kenneth Rasinski, *The Psychology of Survey Response*, Cambridge: Cambridge University Press, 2000.

Tuck, Henry, and Tanya Silverman, *The Counter-Narrative Handbook*, London: Institute for Strategic Dialogue, 2016.

U.S. Agency for International Development, *Voices for Peace*, Washington, D.C., October 2018. As of July 24, 2020:
https://www.usaid.gov/sites/default/files/documents/1860/
Voices_for_Peace_Fact_Sheet_October_2018_KG._BB._Update.pdf

We Are Social, "Digital in 2018 in Southeast Asia," briefing, 2018. As of March 31, 2020:
https://www.slideshare.net/wearesocial/
digital-in-2018-in-southeast-asia-part-2-southeast-86866464

World Bank, "International Migrant Stock (% of Population)—Indonesia," webpage, undated. As of July 21, 2020:
https://data.worldbank.org/indicator/SM.POP.TOTL.ZS?end=2015&locations=ID&start=1990&view=chart